GCLS/GLASSBORO BRANCH
2 CENTER STREET
GLASSBORO, NJ 08028

**A Character Building Book™**

# Learning About Responsibility from the Life of
# Colin Powell

Jeanne Strazzabosco

The Rosen Publishing Group's

**PowerKids Press™**

New York

D1456338

Published in 1996 by The Rosen Publishing Group, Inc.
29 East 21st Street, New York, NY 10010

Copyright © 1996 by The Rosen Publishing Group, Inc.

All rights reserved. No part of this book may be reproduced in any form without permission in writing from the publisher, except by a reviewer.

First Edition

Book design: Erin McKenna

Photo credits: Cover © Archive Photos; p. 8 © Brent Winebrenner/International Stock; p. 11 © Scott Thode/International Stock; all other photos © AP/Wide World Photos.

Strazzabosco, Jeanne.
    Learning about responsibility from the life of Colin Powell / Jeanne Strazzabosco.
        p.   cm. — (A character building book)
    Includes index.
    Summary: Teaches the value of responsibility by taking examples from the life of the African American general Colin Powell.
    ISBN 0-8239-2414-9
    1. Powell, Colin L.—Juvenile literature. 2. Generals—United States—Biography—Juvenile literature. 3. Responsibility—Juvenile literature. [1. Powell, Colin L. 2. Generals. 3. Afro-Americans—Biography. 4. Responsibility.] I. Title. II. Series.
U53.P69S77 1996
355'.0092—dc20
[B]                                              96-24386
                                                  CIP
                                                      AC

Manufactured in the United States of America

# Table of Contents

# Success in America

Colin Luther Powell was born in 1937 in Harlem, New York. His parents had moved to the United States from a country called Jamaica. They believed that if you were **responsible** (ree-SPON-sih-bul), worked hard, and learned as much as you could, you would be **successful** (suk-SES-ful) in the United States. They taught this important idea to Colin.

◀ *Colin, shown here with his wife, Alma, has worked hard to become the success that he is.*

# Working Hard

As a boy, Colin did not like school very much. He did not always do well. But he worked hard. Other students **respected** (ree-SPEK-tid) him. In high school he was **elected** (eh-LEK-tid) class president. He had important positions in several clubs. He knew that if he wanted a good job, he had to go to college. So he did.

*Many people look up to Colin, including this graduate from West Point, the U.S. military* ▶

# The ROTC

One day at college Colin saw an **ROTC** (AR-OH-TEE-SEE) drill team practicing. The ROTC gave students **military** (MIL-ih-tayr-ee) training. When a student completed the program, he could become an officer in the U.S. Army. Colin liked the way the drill team worked together. Colin decided to join his college's ROTC program. From the moment Colin started, he loved it. He liked the physical activity and the **discipline** (DIS-ah-plin) that was required.

◀ *Members of the ROTC work together to learn the skills they need to serve in the armed forces.*

# In the Military

Colin wanted to do well in the ROTC. And he did. He reached the ROTC's highest **rank** (RANK). He graduated from the ROTC at the top of his class. Colin became an officer in the army. He was a second **lieutenant** (loo-TEN-int). Colin worked all over the United States, Europe, South Korea, and Vietnam. He was **confident** (KON-fih-dent), and he worked hard. People knew they could count on him to do a good job. He always planned and thought ahead. He stayed calm. And he was good at solving problems.

*Members of the armed forces are responsible for the safety of the country.* ▶

# Sent to Fight

In 1962, Colin married Alma Johnson. Soon after, he and many other American soldiers were sent to Vietnam. They went to help the South Vietnamese Army. While Colin was there, he stepped in a trap set by the enemy, the North Vietnamese. He hurt his foot so badly that he couldn't walk for a long time. He received a medal called the Purple Heart. He also won a Bronze Star for bravery.

◀ *Colin was a strong leader. His soldiers respected and trusted him.*

# Being Brave

Colin returned to the U.S. He decided that he wanted to move higher up in the Army. He went to the Army's Command and General Staff College. He studied a lot. Once again he graduated at the top of his class.

At that time, more and more American soldiers were fighting in the Vietnam War. Colin was sent back to Vietnam. He pulled a pilot out of a burning helicopter before it exploded. Because he risked his own life, he received a special award called the Soldier's Medal.

*Colin has received many awards during his career in the military.* ▶

# Part of the Government

When Colin returned to the U.S., he wanted to become part of the U.S. **government** (GUH-vern-ment). He went back to school. Two years later he had earned a master's degree. He was also promoted in the Army.

Colin was chosen to be a White House Fellow. As a White House Fellow, it was his **responsibility** (ree-SPON-sih-BIL-ih-tee) to gather information for the President of the United States, Lyndon B. Johnson. Colin knew that the President needed to have the best information possible. He was careful to do a good job.

◄ *Colin worked in the White House for many years.*

# More Responsibility

Next Colin studied at the National War College. He learned about keeping the country safe. He held many important jobs. For two years he had the honor of being a national **security** (seh-KYER-ih-tee) adviser to President Ronald Reagan. It was Colin's responsibility to warn the President about anything that could harm the United States. It is a very difficult job. As always, Colin did his work well. The President knew he could count on Colin to help keep the country safe.

*President Reagan chose Colin for an important position because he knew he could rely on Colin.* ▶

# A Great Leader

In 1989, the Army made Colin a four-star general. President George Bush asked Colin to be the **Chairman** (CHAYR-man) of the Joint Chiefs of Staff. That meant that Colin was the leader of all of the U.S. armed forces. In 1990, Colin ordered the armed forces to go to war in the Persian Gulf. A country called Iraq had invaded another country called Kuwait. Kuwait was an **ally** (AL-ly) of the U.S. So Colin sent the U.S. armed forces to war to stop Iraq. With Colin's help, the U.S. won. Kuwait was safe.

◄ *Colin is highly respected because of the many ways in which he has served his country.*

# Teaching Responsibility

Soon after the Persian Gulf War, Colin **retired** (ree-TYRD) from the Army. He wrote a book about his life. Today he gives speeches all over the country. He talks about his life, his career, and the importance of caring for your country. He is respected by many people. He teaches others what his parents taught him: If you are responsible and work hard, you can be successful.

# Glossary

**ally** (AL-ly)  Country joined with another country for a common goal or reason.

**chairman** (CHAYR-man)  Head or leader of a group.

**confident** (KON-fih-dent)  Trusting in yourself.

**discipline** (DIS-ah-plin)  Training to learn self-control.

**elect** (eh-LEKT)  To choose for a position by voting.

**government** (GUH-vern-ment)  The people who run a country.

**lieutenant** (loo-TEN-int)  A type of officer.

**military** (MIL-ih-tayr-ee)  Having to do with armed forces.

**rank** (RANK)  Official position in the military.

**respect** (ree-SPEKT)  Esteem or admiration.

**responsibility** (ree-SPON-sih-BIL-ih-tee)  Having a duty to do something.

**responsible** (ree-SPON-sih-bul)  Reliable and dependable.

**retire** (ree-TYR)  To leave work after a certain number of years.

**ROTC** (AR-OH-TEE-SEE)  Reserve Officers' Training Corp.

**security** (seh-KYER-ih-tee)  Defense or protection.

**successful** (suk-SES-ful)  To do well.

# Index

Learning about responsibility from the L
J B POWELL STRAZ        32928003142027

Strazzabosco, Jeanne.
GLOUCESTER CO LIBRARY SYSTEM

## DATE DUE

| | | | |
|---|---|---|---|
| FE 03 '98 | | | |
| FE 17 '98 | | | |
| MR 03 '98 | | | |
| AG 24 '98 | | | |
| FE 26 '00 | | | |
| AUG 22 | | | |
| MR 10 '00 | | | |
| DE 10 '01 | | | |
| | | | |
| | | | |
| | | | |
| | | | |
| | | | |
| | | | |
| | | | |

DEMCO 38-296

♡

I love you